Regulated Relaxation

Mindfully Navigating Financial Markets

Table of Contents

Chapter 1. Introduction

In this Special Report titled "Regulated Relaxation: Mindfully Navigating Financial Markets", we unravel not just the secrets of the financial markets but also guide you on fostering mindfulness amidst its intricate maze. Despite the markets being a battleground of highs and lows, we believe that a calm, centered approach can make the journey more rewarding. Inside, we demystify the mechanics of trading and investing, but more importantly, we help you master the art of mindfully engaging with financial spectacles. If you've ever felt intrigued by the financial world yet overwhelmed by its volatility, this report has been curate just for you. Get ready to venture into an exciting expedition where finance meets mindfulness, potentially transforming your financial prowess and personal serenity. The report promises a joyful reading experience designed to equip, enlighten, and embolden your path to financial well-being. Rest assured, this isn't just another financial guide; it is your wholesome companion for a mindful financial journey. Hurry, grab your exclusive copy today, and embark on a voyage towards regulated relaxation in the financial seascape.

Chapter 2. Unveiling Financial Markets: A Comprehensive Overview

The financial markets—a vast, intricate web of institutions, investors, and mechanisms—are a cardinal part of any economy. Perhaps their most impressive aspect is their ceaseless ability to breathe life into businesses, fueling growth and prosperity. Yet, their complex nature often masks many truths from the untrained eye. This chapter brings into focus the true ethos of financial markets, unravelling their multifaceted nature, and explaining their profound influence over the economic tapestry.

2.1. Understanding the Core of Financial Markets

Financial markets are arenas where people trade financial securities and derivatives at prices that reflect supply and demand. Banks, insurance companies, pension funds, professional traders – they all converge here, armed with diverse financial instruments.

The markets can be physical (stock exchange on Wall Street) or virtual (an electronic network such as the NASDAQ), facilitating the purchase and sale of securities, currencies, commodities, and other financial assets. Furthermore, they are categorized by the types of securities sold and the nature of transactions.

2.2. Primary and Secondary Markets: Dual Facets of a Singular System

Financial markets are segmented into primary and secondary markets. In the primary market, new securities are issued for the first time. When a company needs money for growth, it may sell part of its equity or issue debt to investors—this fundraising process happens in the primary market.

On the other hand, the secondary market deals with the subsequent trading of securities initially issued in the primary market. This is where most of us engage as investors, buying and selling shares of companies through various stock exchanges and electronic systems.

2.3. Different Types of Financial Markets

There are diverse types of financial markets, each serving a unique function and catering to different investor requirements. Let's delve deeper:

1. ***Stock Market***: The stock market allows companies to raise capital and investors to become partial owners of those companies. Stocks represent a claim on part of the company's assets and earnings.

2. ***Bond Market***: Also known as the debt or credit market, it is where investors lend money for a certain period at a variable or fixed interest rate. Governments and businesses use this market to raise funds for various reasons.

3. ***Commodities Market***: Here, buyers and sellers trade commodities such as gold, oil, wheat or sugar. Traditional

commodity markets facilitated physical exchange of goods, but today, most transactions are virtual.

4. ***Derivatives Market***: In this market, parties enter contracts to buy or sell an asset at a future date at a price agreed upon today. These contracts are derived from underlying assets like stocks, bonds, commodities, currencies, interest rates, or even market indexes.

5. ***Foreign Exchange Market (Forex Market)***: In Forex, currencies are exchanged. It's the most liquid financial market, given its enormous trading volume and continuous operation, encompassing everything from a tourist swapping currencies to billion-dollar transactions made by global corporations and governments.

2.4. Influencing Factors: What Moves the Market

Understanding the forces that drive financial markets is crucial to navigating them effectively. Key factors affecting market conditions include:

1. ***Interest Rates***: Lower interest rates encourage borrowing and investing, potentially boosting market activity, while higher rates slow borrowing and can dampen market enthusiasm.

2. ***Economic Indicators***: Key indicators, such as GDP, inflation rates, unemployment rates, manufacturing output, affect investor sentiment and, consequently, market movements.

3. ***Political Stability and Regulatory Changes***: National political stability, upcoming elections, changes in government policies, and regulations can induce significant market volatility.

4. ***Market Sentiment***: Investor emotions can impact markets significantly. Fear or optimism can lead to sell-offs or buying sprees, respectively.

5. ***Corporate Earnings and News***: A company's performance and the release of important news can influence individual stocks and, in turn, the overall market.

2.5. Conclusion: A Complex Yet Essential Mechanism

While financial markets might appear complicated and unwieldy, they are essential to a well-functioning economy. They determine the price of securities, helping to manage and control risk while providing a platform for investors and businesses to meet.

However, this complex arena does not come without its hazards. While potentially lucrative, the financial markets can be challenging to navigate – market hazards warrant caution, and rewards should be sought mindfully. Take this understanding as a cornerstone upon which to build your investment strategy and traverse the financial journey that lies ahead.

Chapter 3. Understanding Volatility: The Art and Science

In the world of finance, volatility refers to the degree of variation seen in the price of a financial instrument over time. Understanding this concept and learning to navigate it effectively can significantly impact your financial journey. Let's start this exploration by defining volatility more precisely and inspecting its implications.

3.1. Understanding the Concept of Volatility

Volatility often serves as a measure of uncertainty or risk associated with the size of changes in an asset's values. More substantial variation in price signifies higher volatility, meaning more extensive leaps between high and low values. In this context, understanding volatility equates exploring risk, uncertainty, and variability in the financial markets.

There are two types of volatility: historical and implied. Historical volatility assesses the fluctuations of a security's price in the past, allowing traders to forecast future behavior. On the other hand, implied volatility, often measured by indicators like the VIX, represents market expectations of future volatility.

Volatility plays a critical role in defining both strategy and outlook with investment and trading decisions. For example, in the options market, high volatility usually increases option premiums due to potentially larger price swings, making psychology and emotions an essential aspect of trading.

3.2. Tools for Tracking Volatility

While the concept of volatility may seem abstract, several tools can aid in measuring and understanding it.

One of the most commonly used measures is the Volatility Index (VIX), also known as the "fear-gauge". This index tracks implied volatility of S&P 500 index options, showcasing market expectations for the next 30-day period.

Another popular tool for checking the volatility of individual stocks is the Average True Range (ATR), providing valuable information on how much a security's price is moving each day on average.

3.3. The Science: Volatility and Probability Distributions

From a scientific standpoint, volatility often conforms to specific statistical models. The most frequently used model for financial data is the log-normal distribution. This model enables deriving sophisticated measures like the 'Value at Risk' metric, correlating risk and volatility directly.

There are also more complex models like the GARCH model, primarily used for time-series financial data, treating volatility as a random variable. These models point to the probability of price movements, indicating possible future outcomes.

3.4. The Art: Harnessing Volatility Mindfully

Beyond the data and probability distributions lies the art of dealing with volatility. This art is deeply tethered to mindfulness and emotional regulation. Volatility can evoke strong emotions; hence, cultivating an ability to observe these emotions without being swept up in them is essential.

One mindfulness tool for this is anchoring — deliberately focusing on a neutral or positive sensation to stabilize the mind amidst market volatility. For instance, concentrating on your breath or the sensation of your feet on the ground can help bring more emotional clarity.

Another strategy is to foster an attitude of curiosity towards volatility instead of fear, thereby shifting your perspective from risk-averse to potentially risk-welcoming.

3.5. Managing Volatility in Investment Portfolios

In the realm of investing, managing volatility translates into portfolio diversification and risk management. It means spreading investments across various assets, sectors or geographical regions to reduce exposure to a single volatile asset. Here, the key is to strike a balance between potential returns and risk level.

Risk management tools like stop-loss orders also come into play to limit potential losses from highly volatile assets. These tools protect by selling an asset when its price falls to a specific level.

3.6. Viewing Volatility as an Ally

Shifting the lens through which one views volatility is where finance truly meets mindfulness. Instead of perceiving volatility as purely risk, viewing it as an opportunity invites a new set of possibilities.

High volatility often presents chances to buy assets at discounted prices. Moreover, a volatile market can lead to lucrative return potentials for those who can identify and act on these opportunities while keeping their composure.

By honing emotional intelligence and mindfulness, one can maneuver through market volatility with greater grace, turning what seems like a turbulent journey into a dance with the market's rhythm.

In a nutshell, understanding volatility is to comprehend the cyclical and ever-changing nature of markets. It serves not just as an essential element of financial literacy but is also linked to personal growth. By acknowledging the presence of uncertainty, we can make more informed decisions and navigate financial markets with wisdom and serenity.

Chapter 4. Judicious Risk-Taking: A Balanced Perspective

Every journey, whether in life or in finance, carries a level of risk. In navigating the financial markets, the concept of risk is further magnified by the realm's inherent unpredictability and complexity. Inextricably linked to potential rewards, risks are the stumbling blocks that can either propel or hamper an investor's journey. The ability to judiciously handle risk is like a compass guiding you towards safe investment shores. It requires understanding, patience, and above all, the art of mental equanimity.

Understanding risk forms the keystone without which a solid investment foundation cannot be built. As Benjamin Graham, the father of value investing, once wisely stated: "The essence of investment management is the management of risks, not the management of returns."

4.1. Understanding Risk

To deal effectively with risk, one must first understand its many facets and derivatives. Financial risk can manifest in several ways — it could be a market risk where the entire market takes a dip leading to lowered asset values, or it could be a credit risk where the borrower defaults on their payments. Again, it could be a liquidity risk where certain assets fail to convert into cash quickly enough to meet urgent financial needs.

Interestingly, risk isn't always synonymous with loss. Risk in essence encapsulates uncertainty which can swing both ways, resulting in either profit or loss. By understanding this, you approach the financial markets not as a perilous minefield, but as a playing field where calculations and decisions can shift the odds in your favor.

4.2. The Risk-Reward Spectrum

Every investment opportunity lies somewhere on the risk-reward spectrum. On one end, investments like government bonds might offer lower returns, but they present minute risk. On the other end, investments such as startup equity may promise astronomical returns but invariably come with significant risk. As an investor, understanding where exactly on this risk-reward continuum your investment lies is critical.

There is no one-size-fits-all approach to this. An investment strategy that works for one individual may not work for another. Factors such as financial goals, age, income level, investment horizon, and risk tolerance determine where on the spectrum an investor should ideally position themselves.

4.3. Risk Evaluation Tools

Numerous tools exist to aid investors in their quest to understand and assess risk. The standard deviation is one such tool that helps measure the level of price volatility, providing insights into how much an investment's returns can deviate from its expected returns.

The Beta of a security is another useful metric, offering a snapshot of how much risk a specific security presents in relation to the overall market. A beta greater than 1 indicates that the security is more volatile than the market, and vice versa.

The Sharpe Ratio, formulated by Nobel laureate William F. Sharpe, compares risk-adjusted returns, allowing investors to understand how much return is achieved for each unit of risk taken. Using such tools, investors can be better positioned to understand and manage their risk.

4.4. Risk Mitigation Strategies

Having recognized the types, measurements, and tools associated with risk, the next step lies in devising risk mitigation strategies. These may include diversification, where one spreads their investment across a variety of assets to hedge against the underperformance of a particular sector or asset class. Another strategy is hedging through derivatives like futures and options, which can offer a safety net against potential losses.

Investors should also maintain an emergency fund and be cautious about leveraging or borrowing to invest, as it may amplify potential losses.

Risk management further extends to keeping emotions in check, adopting a long-term perspective, and not being swayed by short-term market fluctuations or hype. By taking a mindful approach, you can curiously observe market patterns and make considered decisions, rather than being driven by fear or greed.

4.5. The Power of Mindfulness in Risk Taking

Often the biggest risk one faces in investing isn't market volatility, inflation, or liquidity threats, but the investor's own mind. Mental biases can lead to irrational decisions causing potential harm to the investment portfolio. It's here that mindfulness steps in, enabling inner equilibrium in the face of risk.

This doesn't imply watching from the sidelines, but actively participating in the financial dance, mindfully aware of every step you take. Practicing mindfulness can help you cultivate a balanced perspective towards risk, neutralizing the fear of losses and the allure of quick gains. Investment decisions then arise not from a whirlwind of emotions, but from a calm, clear judgment grounded in careful thought and understanding.

This chapter's journey started with the notion of risk and now concludes with a perspective - to mindfully perceive risk as an inherent element of the financial landscape, an element that can be managed, mitigated, and at times, even embraced. As you imbibe mindfulness in your financial journey, remember that judicious risk-taking isn't just about securing financial rewards, but also about cherishing the invaluable rewards of personal growth and learning that the journey offers. Through mindfulness, you shift from being a mere participant in the financial markets to becoming a balanced navigator, mindfully charting your own course amidst the exhilarating waves of the financial seascape.

Chapter 5. Mindfulness: Why it Matters in Finance

Many financial experts emphasize the tangible aspects of finance, such as asset allocation, risk management, and market analysis, often neglecting an integral part of the equation—the individual. With that in mind, let's delve deeper into understanding the importance of mindfulness and why it matters in the world of finance.

5.1. The Concept of Mindfulness

Mindfulness is a state of active, open attention to the present. This awareness incorporates the acceptance of thoughts, emotions, and physical sensations without judgment or distraction. By observing what transpires in one's mind and body without getting engrossed in it, you gain a heightened sense of clarity and perception.

[[.example]]

> The experience could be likened to watching a film from the director's viewpoint. Instead of getting absorbed in the narrative or characters, you're observing the broader picture—comprehending the plot while appreciating the nuances, like lighting effects or camera angles.

Just as mindfulness has its roots in meditation and spiritual practice, its significance extends beyond the personal sphere into various professional arenas, including finance.

5.2. Mindfulness in the Financial Realm

There's an adage that states, "Personal finance is more personal than it is finance." This essentially means the individual's psychology, habits, and emotional triggers often dictate financial decisions more than market trends or financial data. This underrecognized element significantly impacts investment decisions and long-term financial planning. Therefore, the cultivation of awareness and clarity through mindfulness becomes crucial in financial decision-making.

The financial realm, with its volatility, can easily stimulate anxiety, fear, and other strong emotions, adversely affecting decisions and actions. However, a mindful approach equips you with the skill set to navigate through these impulses, fostering thoughtful decision-making and improved financial outcomes.

5.3. The Science Behind Mindfulness

Studies in neuroscience and psychology have provided empirical evidence that mindfulness practice rewires the neural framework, enhancing cognition, decision-making, and emotional regulation. These enhancements effectively translate into better financial habits and improved investment decisions.

When one is mindful, it triggers the 'executive function' of the brain located in the prefrontal cortex. This area is responsible for rational thinking and decision-making. On the other hand, reactive decisions are often driven by the amygdala—the region of the brain associated with emotions. Hence, by bolstering the executive function, mindfulness facilitates higher rationality and lower impulsivity in decision-making—a vital trait for managing finances successfully.

[[.example]]

Think of this as having a calm and thoughtful captain steering your financial ship, as opposed to an impulsive, panic-prone sailor.

5.4. Mindfulness and Investment Decisions

The art of investing typically entails dealing with uncertainty, making informed predictions, and managing risks. This process inherently generates stress and emotional reactions. An investor's actions can be significantly dictated by the fluctuations of the market and their emotional reactions to these changes, which might lead to hasty, suboptimal decisions.

Mindfulness, with its emphasis on acceptance and non-judgment, encourages investors to view market fluctuations objectively, without the lens of fear or greed. It trains the investor to understand their emotional triggers and gradually detach from them, ensuring decisions are driven by logic rather than emotion.

Additionally, mindfulness engenders patience and long-term thinking—key tenets for successful investing. By cultivating acceptance of the present moment, mindfulness reduces the urge for immediate gratification, enabling investors to stick to their investment strategy irrespective of short-term market vicissitudes.

5.5. Mindfulness and Financial Habits

Apart from shaping investment decisions, mindfulness impacts general financial habits too, such as saving, budgeting, and spending.

For instance, mindful budgeting encourages conscious understanding of where your money goes, appreciating the utility it provides and discerning needs from wants. This awareness can bring remarkable changes to spending habits, helping curb impulsive shopping and promoting value-oriented expenditure.

Likewise, mindful saving benefits from this enhanced self-awareness. By understanding the emotional aspect behind spending, one can choose to save instead, working towards long-term financial goals without feeling deprived.

5.6. Cultivating Mindfulness in Finance

Even with the understanding of mindfulness and its impact, how does one cultivate it in the realm of finance?

Various practices like mindful meditation, journaling, and breathing exercises can provide a foundation. Incorporating these habits into your routine can offer a general sense of mindfulness that can be then applied to finance. However, it's crucial to consciously bring this awareness to your financial activities—be it evaluating a potential investment, budgeting, or even everyday spending decisions.

To recap, mindfulness' importance in finance lies in its ability to foster clarity, enhance perception, and regulate emotional reactions, thereby transforming financial decision-making. By integrating mindfulness into your financial practice, you can navigate the waves of the financial market with composure and wisdom, achieving not just monetary gains but personal growth and peace. Mindfulness in finance, therefore, offers an unexplored vista of conscious financial well-being.

Chapter 6. The Psychology of Financial Decision Making

Just as the human mind adjusts and reacts to countless stimuli and external factors daily, traders' and investors' decision making processes adjust and react to the constant ebb and flow of financial markets. Before we delve into the intricacies of trading psychology, let's understand the components of financial decision making.

6.1. Understanding Financial Decision Making

Financial decision-making is a blend of various components: a trader's individual psychology, their response to market information, the process of decision-making itself, and the subsequent execution of a trading plan. When navigating the financial sea, several psychological factors twist and turn our thought processes, inevitably impact decisions. There is a unique interaction and a push-and-pull dynamic between emotions and rational thinking. Let's examine some core psychological elements.

6.2. The Emotion-Rationality Nexus

Understandably, financial decisions are impacted by emotions - fear, greed, hope, and regret all come to play. While emotions can provide valuable insights, unchecked feelings can distort rational thinking and cloud judgment. Conversely, cold logic and pure rationality might not necessarily always lead to the most beneficial financial outcomes.

Fear can lead to panic selling, while greed can entice an investor to hold onto positions longer than warranted. As an investor, identifying emotional triggers, understanding the root causes, and developing mechanisms to manage and mitigate their impacts is crucial.

6.3. Cognitive Biases in Financial Decision Making

A significant component of psychology in financial decision-making pertains to cognitive biases. These mental shortcuts or 'heuristics' help us cope with a complex world. However, they can also lead us astray when making financial decisions. Here are a few relevant biases:

- **Confirmation bias**: We tend to favor information that confirms our existing beliefs or theories.

- **Recency bias**: Our decisions are heavily influenced by the most recent information.

- **Availability bias**: We base decisions on information that's readily available rather than complete facts.

- **Anchoring bias**: Here, individuals anchor their opinions to a reference point—even if it's irrelevant to the decision at hand.

- **Overconfidence bias**: The tendency to overestimate our abilities, which can lead to excessive risk-taking.

A successful participant in the financial market is aware of these biases, understands their impact, and takes steps to mitigate them.

6.4. The Influence of Behavioral Finance

Behavioral finance is a field that marries the study of psychology with traditional finance to provide explanations for why people make irrational financial decisions. It posits that investors are not always rational, have limits to their self-control, and are influenced by their own biases. Behavioral finance studies the effects of psychological, social, cognitive, and emotional factors on the financial decisions of individuals and institutions and how those decisions vary from those implied by traditional finance.

The introduction of concepts such as 'prospect theory' or 'loss aversion' have refined our understanding of financial decision-making. Prospect theory suggests that people decide between probabilistic alternatives based on potential gains and losses, not final outcomes. Loss aversion signifies a strong tendency to prefer avoiding losses than acquiring gains.

6.5. Building Mindfulness in Financial Decision Making

Mindfulness involves becoming aware of one's thoughts and feelings without getting caught up in them. It helps us identify potential pitfalls in our thought process, recognize cognitive biases, and manage our emotional responses effectively. By practicing mindfulness, traders can create a psychological edge, leading to improved decision-making capabilities.

Mindfulness can be built through various techniques, such as meditation, focused exercise, or even simple routines like mindful eating. The key lies in consistent practice and conscious application of these learned mindfulness techniques when navigating financial landscapes.

To summarize, the psychology behind financial decision-making is multifactorial, complex, and influenced not just by the investor's psyche but also by their surrounding environment. Understanding and practicing mindfulness can significantly contribute to improving our biases and emotional responses, leading to effective decision-making. Remember, the voyage through the financial seascape becomes less daunting when we are more aware, mindful, and intentional about our decisions.

Chapter 7. Stress and Financial Markets: Breaking the Connection

The juxtaposition of ideation and reality is particularly vivid when it comes to the sphere of financial markets. Many people, lured by the theoretical profitability, often neglect an existential component of these markets—the stress they engender. In this discourse, we will explore the relationships between stress, the financial markets, and how to navigate these tumultuous waters mindfully, thus breaking the connection resulting in distress.

7.1. Understanding Stress in Financial Markets

We begin with a straightforward question: "What is stress?". Stress, in general terms, is a feeling of emotional or physical tension that comes from any event or thought inducing a feeling of frustration, anger, or nervousness. In the financial markets, stress springs from the uncertainties, the dramatic shifts, and the highs and lows that form an intrinsic part of this arena. Being reactive to these market conditions often leads to unhealthy stress levels, adversely impacting not only your financial decision-making capacity but also your overall well-being.

Financial stress can manifest in many forms: the anxiety of investment performance, fear of loss, the pressure to fulfill financial goals, or simply the vastness of the market itself. It becomes essential to acknowledge this stress first, only then can one work towards alleviating it.

7.2. Stress: The Unseen Enemy

Stress has long been painted as a silent destroyer. Chronic stress impacts various facets of our life and has been linked to numerous health issues such as heart diseases, depression, and a weakened immune system. Within the financial world, it can sabotage your decision-making skills, causing hasty actions and fogging clear judgement. As a result, instead of thoughtful, informed decisions, you might start making emotionally charged choices. This can create a vicious cycle: poor decisions leading to financial loss, thereby boosting stress, and further impeding sensible choices.

The first line of defense against this unseen enemy is understanding the sources of stress and acknowledging its presence. Once acknowledged, the beast can be tamed.

7.3. Mindfulness: The Stress Buster

Mindfulness, a form of meditative practice rooted in Eastern philosophies, has made its way to Western mental health discussions. Now, it has further seeped into the realm of finance. At its core, mindfulness encourages living in the present, being attentive, and accepting one's thoughts and feelings without judgment.

When applied to the financial markets, mindfulness helps you to handle market volatility not with fear and panic, but with a sense of calm and rationality. Awareness of the present market scenario, detached from any past losses or future anxieties, can significantly lower your stress levels and allow for more meaningful decisions.

In a sphere ruled by numbers and dramatized by unpredictable scenarios, mindfulness can be a beacon of tranquility and control.

7.4. Techniques to Cultivate Financial Mindfulness

Now that we've laid out the theoretical foundation, let's move towards the practical applications of mindfulness in the realm of finance:

- Daily Reflections: Journaling your thoughts and feelings about the market conditions can help in gaining insights about your emotional triggers and equips you to manage them better. Similarly, maintaining a trading journal documenting your trades, reasons, and results can provide an objective perspective of your trading methods, highlighting areas of improvements and strengths.

- Mindful Meditation: Regular practice of mindful meditation can train your mind to stay focused and not get swayed by the market's changing dynamics. Simple breathing exercises are a good place to start. Take a few moments, let your body relax, and focus solely on your breath. With time, you can explore advanced meditation techniques.

- Cultivate Patience: Good returns take time. Rushing into trades or investments, driven by the fear of missing out (FOMO), can lead to unnecessary stress. Adopt a slow and steady approach. Be patient with your trades and investments.

Remember, the primary goal is not just to make well-informed financial decisions but also to enjoy the process. When you align yourself with the present moment in the financial markets, stress starts losing its grip, leading to 'Regulated Relaxation'.

7.5. Concluding Thoughts

It is pertinent to note that stress is not always harmful. A certain level of stress known as 'eustress' could promote growth, inspire creativity, and motivate you to reach your goals. However, it becomes problematic when it tips over to chronic stress, hindering your capacity to think clearly and make optimal financial decisions.

Breaking the connection between stress and financial markets doesn't imply eliminating stress altogether but instead channelling it to work in your favor. The journey starts with acknowledgment, treads through the path of mindfulness, and ultimately leads to regulated relaxation.

Our financial journey will undoubtedly have its share of storms and calm waters. Our prime endeavor should be to equip ourselves with the tools of mindfulness, enabling us to steer our ship steadily, irrespective of the weather. By doing so, not only do we reach our financial goals, but we also enable a journey filled with peace, composure, and serene satisfaction. The financial seascape, which once seemed daunting, gradually transforms into a realm of regulated relaxation.

Through relentless practice, what once seemed to be an intrinsic link between the stress and financial markets begins to wane, replaced by a mindful navigator. You then operate not from a place of anxiety or fear, but from a place of calm and centered strength. In this process, one learns that while the markets' crests and troughs are beyond your control, your responses to them are within your authority. By accepting this, we make the first step towards a mindful financial journey.

Chapter 8. Emotional Intelligence: Mastering Your Financial Emotions

To navigate the stormy sea of financial markets, one must master their vessel - not just the tools and techniques, but also the often-overlooked part of managing the ship: the emotional intelligence. We begin by understanding what exactly emotional intelligence is and how it applies to our financial journey.

8.1. Understanding Emotional Intelligence

Emotional Intelligence (EI), often measured as an Emotional Intelligence Quotient (EQ), is the aptitude to identify, interpret, and manage both our emotions and the emotions of others. EI encompasses four key pillars: self-awareness, self-regulation, empathy, and social skill.

Understanding these components is the first step towards mastering your financial emotions. We'll delve into these in the following sections and explore how they translate into the financial domain.

8.2. The Pillars of Emotional Intelligence and Their Financial Correlates

8.2.1. Self Awareness: Knowing Your Financial Temperament

Self-awareness refers to our ability to recognize our emotions as they occur and understand their effect on our thoughts and behavior. Transferring this concept to the financial world, it implies understanding your reactions to various market situations.

Does the sight of red, indicating falling share prices, make you anxious? Or does it come across as an opportunity to buy? Does a bull market put you in overconfidence, potentially leading to hasty decisions? Recognizing such emotional responses can be instrumental in financial decisions.

8.2.2. Self Regulation: Controlled Financial Decision Making

The ability to regulate our emotional reactions constitutes the next pillar. When moved by market volatility, can you stop yourself from panic selling or greedy buying? This self-regulation in financial decisions makes a crucial difference between successful investors and those who get swept away by market tides.

8.2.3. Empathy: Understanding the Market Mood

On a broad level, empathy is understanding others' emotions. In a financial context, it may not necessarily refer to individuals but rather intuiting the mood of the market. Successful investors often have a knack for anticipating market trends, not just through charts and figures but by reading subtle cues on investor sentiment, economic factors, and global events affecting the business environment.

8.2.4. Social Skill: Collaborative Financial Success

Lastly, social skill, which involves managing relationships and building networks, can open doors to more investment opportunities, learning from mentors, or working with financial advisors. Fostering these relationships also allows for diverse perspectives, collaborative decision-making, and shared risks and rewards.

8.3. Implementing Emotional Intelligence in Financial Decisions

Now that we have outlined the importance of emotional intelligence and its financial correlates let's discuss a few practical steps to implement EI in your financial journey.

8.3.1. Create an Emotional Journal

Record your emotions during various market trends, and over time, you'll develop an understanding of your emotional patterns in response to financial upturns and downturns.

8.3.2. Practice Mindful Investing

Mindful investing involves making decisions based not on impulsive emotional reactions but thoughtful contemplation. One way to do this is by following a predetermined investment strategy and not deviating from it due to market sentiments.

8.3.3. Develop Emotional Resilience

Market volatility is inevitable. Building emotional resilience enables you to stay peaceful amidst economic upheavals, allowing you to take calculated risks and make sound judgments.

8.3.4. Build Constructive Financial Relationships

A shared financial journey often paves the way for holistic growth. While a mentor can provide guidance based on their experience, peers offer support and fresh perspectives.

In conclusion, the journey to financial success isn't just about understanding the market; it's equally about understanding oneself. When you master your financial emotions through emotional intelligence, the seemingly overwhelming financial markets no longer intimidate, but invite, rewarding you with not just economic gains but personal growth and peace of mind.

Chapter 9. Sensible Investing: Mind Over Markets

Investing sensibly requires more than just an understanding of the financial markets; it also demands a mindful approach. This unique interplay of mindfulness and investment strategies can empower you to make informed yet confident decisions, despite the ever-changing economic landscape.

9.1. Understanding Mindful Investing

Mindful investing is a unique approach that combines investment principles with mindfulness techniques. It involves not only understanding the intricacies of the financial markets but also consciously cultivating a focused, unbiased, and serene mindset. Mindfulness can provide a solid foundation for sensible investing.

Mindful investing means being fully aware of every decision you make, being in tune with changes in the market, and calmly analyzing your reactions to these shifts. It's about understanding that fear and greed, the two most powerful emotions in the investing world, can distort your decision-making process.

A key component of mindful investing is maintaining an ability to remain detached, witnessing market fluctuations without being tossed around by them. It involves cultivating an ability to respond thoughtfully rather than react impulsively. Essentially, mindful investing is maintaining a state of relaxed alertness in the face of financial market's endless stream of uncertainties.

9.2. The Salience of Diversification and Portfolio Management

Diversification has proven to be a critical strategy in managing risk while investing. Mindful diversification involves spreading your investments across a variety of assets to protect against the volatility of any single investment.

A diversified portfolio could include a mix of stocks, bonds, commodities, and cash equivalents. To manage this portfolio mindfully, regularly review and rebalance your portfolio to keep aligned with your goals.

Mindful portfolio management also involves the application of mindfulness techniques in executing your investment strategy. One such technique is active acceptance. In the context of portfolio management, active acceptance can mean acknowledging the presence of risk, though it doesn't mean tolerating imprudent risks. Remember that losses are part of the journey and using them to learn and adjust your strategy is an act of mindfulness.

9.3. Reactive vs. Proactive Investing

Reactive investing is an approach wherein investors react to market events and trends, whereas proactive investing involves making decisions based on extensive research and planning.

In reactive investing, decisions are often influenced by emotions which lead to ill-timed buys and sells. This establishes a pattern of buying high and selling low—the exact opposite of a sound investment strategy.

On the contrary, proactive investing involves setting clear, calculated goals and creating a well-structured plan. Employing mindfulness in proactive investing allows for a careful evaluation of the situation and making deliberate, well-informed decisions rather than knee-jerk reactions.

9.4. The Art of Patience in Investing

Patience is one of the most critical virtues in the world of investing. It allows you to stay the course during moments of extreme volatility and uncertainty.

Mindful investing offers a structured approach to cultivate patience. Mindful practices like meditation can counteract stress and help investors stay calm, enabling them to make logical decisions.

Practicing patience doesn't mean sitting idle. It involves careful analysis, knowing when to take action, and when to maintain restraint—a balance between activity and passivity, always keeping an eye on the long-term perspective.

9.5. Case Studies: Lessons from Successful Investors

Finally, let's draw insights from successful investors who have incorporated mindfulness into their investment strategies.

- Warren Buffet, the 'Oracle of Omaha,' emphasizes staying calm and patient, advocating a long-term strategic approach to investing rather than a reactive one. He firmly believes that "the stock market is designed to transfer money from the active to the patient."

- Ray Dalio, the founder of Bridgewater Associates, a prominent global hedge fund, incorporates transcendental meditation into his daily routine, believing it improves his clarity and decision-making ability.

We can take note of incorporating mindfulness practices in our investment regime and reap its benefits in managing our financial well-being.

In closing, the integration of mindfulness into our investment practices fosters an environment of calm and collected decision making. Mindful investing allows us to navigate the turbulent waters of the financial markets with equanimity and poise. Through sensible investing, we promote a balanced approach, taking advantage of market opportunities while being mindful of the inherent risks. It encourages us to accept and learn from our mistakes, elevating our investing acumen, and enhancing our overall journey towards financial well-being.

Chapter 10. Practicing Mindfulness in Financial Debacles: Staying Afloat

Financial debacles, precisely because of the intense emotions they trigger, give us an unparalleled opportunity to practice mindfulness. By developing a posture of curiosity and non-judgment, we can transform these occasions of financial stress into moments of insight and personal growth.

10.1. The Nature of Financial Debacles

A financial debacle can take many forms. It could be a catastrophic market crash, a failed investment, or any significant financial setback. No matter the situation, the emotions triggered are almost universally intense - panic, fear, regret, remorse. In these moments, mindfulness may seem unrealistic; however, it is precisely in these moments of stress that mindfulness can be most beneficial.

Mindfulness encourages us to face challenging situations with an attitude of curiosity and openness, free from judgment. It invites us to step back and witness our experiences rather than being consumed by them, fostering clarity and composure in the heat of chaos.

10.2. Mindfulness Practice amidst Market Volatility

Financial markets are, by their nature, volatile. As an investor, you will occasionally experience downturns and losses. While these aren't easy times, they do present a distinctive opportunity to grow both as an individual and as an investor through the practice of mindfulness.

During periods of market downturn, the first mindfulness practice to utilize is mindful observation. This involves observing your thoughts and feelings about the market downturn without trying to change or avoid them. It's acknowledging that fear and anxiety are a natural response to the situation. As you become aware of your internal reactions, you may notice habitual patterns of thinking that contribute to your stress.

Another mindfulness practice useful during such times is grounded breathing. When the markets are in a downward spiral and anxiety levels are high, turn to your breath. Practice slow, deep belly breathing, focusing on the sensation of the breath in your body. Grounded breathing helps to anchor you in the present moment, providing an island of calm in the tumultuous sea of financial markets.

The practice of mindful acceptance is also highly beneficial during times of financial upheaval. This involves accepting what you cannot change about the situation. As an investor, you can't control market performance. However, practicing mindful acceptance allows you to focus your energy on what you do have control over, like your financial decisions and attitudes.

10.3. Resilience and Financial Decision Making

Emotional resilience, which is a by-product of mindfulness, is key in financial decision-making, especially during debacles. It pertains to your ability to bounce back from stressful or even traumatizing events while maintaining your composure.

Resilience is instrumental in mitigating the negative impact of financial losses and reframing them as opportunities for learning. By accepting financial loss with tranquility and realizing its inevitability, investors can better control their reactions and make more sound financial decisions.

Financial decisions made in a mindful state, where emotions take a back seat, tend to be more strategic and result-oriented. It's all about ensuring that sentiments don't cloud judgement and investing decisions are based on sound principles and long-term goals.

10.4. Fostering Emotional Intelligence: A Key Aspect of Mindfulness

Mindfulness promotes Emotional Intelligence (EI), which can be a valuable tool in navigating financial debacles. EI involves recognizing, understanding, and managing our own emotions and the emotions of others.

Knowing when and why you are stressed, angry, or scared is important during a financial crisis, and mindfulness helps us in exactly this aspect. By being able to identify the emotions at play, you can create some psychological space around those emotions to prevent them from spilling over into your decision-making process.

EI also allows you to differentiate between temporary market volatility and times when market trends signal it's time to reassess your investment strategy. This discernment, fostered by mindfulness, can lead to smarter investment decisions.

10.5. Conclusion: Mindfulness as a Financial Ally

In conclusion, mindfulness can act as a guiding light in the darkest times of financial tumult. It not only equips you with more awareness about your psychological states but also assists you in making a more measured response to market volatility.

Remember, the road to financial well-being is lined with peaks and valleys, gains and losses. Rather than being a deterrent, these fluctuations are opportunities for developing mindfulness, resilience, and ultimately, the chance to become a more enlightened investor. By practicing mindfulness, you take the reins of your financial journey, steering it confidently through both fair and stormy weather.

Through our exploration of mindfulness in financial debacles, we've seen that mindfulness isn't just a tool for self-improvement in the traditional sense; it's a potent strategy for financial well-being. By developing a mindful attitude towards financial crises, you can foster resilience, make sound financial decisions, cultivate emotional intelligence, and, ultimately, stay afloat during the toughest financial challenges.

Chapter 11. Case Studies: Successful Mindful Navigation of Financial Markets

The ability to tranquilly navigate the turbulence of financial markets requires both a deep understanding of economic fundamentals and a mindful approach to mitigating stress. The people and organizations featured in the following case studies exemplify this, having demonstrated an impressive economic insight and exceptional mindfulness practice.

11.1. Story of Warren Buffet's Mindful Approach

Warren Buffett, also known as the "Oracle of Omaha," is synonymous with successful investing. His initial company, Berkshire Hathaway, has made many people millionaires due to its consistently impressive performance.

Underneath the numbers, however, is a practice of mindfulness. Buffett's investment strategy leans heavily on intrinsic valuation - evaluating a company based on its real, inherent worth rather than its current market price. His approach involves thorough research into a company's business model, market position, and future growth potential. He considers the current market value as a reference, but makes decisions primarily driven by his understanding of the company's value.

Buffet's measured approach to investing is a direct reflection of his mindfulness practice. Rather than reacting impulsively to market fluctuations, Buffett chooses to remain calm, centered, and focused on the long game. His ability to maintain a sense of detachment from the hype and panic that often grip the financial markets is an exemplar of mindful navigation.

11.2. Vanguard Group: Keeping Calm in the Storm

The Vanguard Group is an investment advisor with more than $5.3 trillion in assets under management. Much of the company's massive success can be attributed to its embrace of mindfulness and long-term strategic thinking.

Founder John C. Bogle was a pioneer of index investing, which is based around the idea that most investors, due to bad timing or poor stock selection, can't outperform the broader market. Vanguard's investment style involves buying and holding an index—an entire market or sector—through a mutual fund or an exchange-traded fund.

Mindfulness is woven into Vanguard's business model. The company recognizes that chasing market trends often leads to poor decision-making. Instead, they've committed to remaining focused on their long-term strategy, undeterred by the increasingly fast pace of the market.

11.3. Ray Dalio: Implementing Radical Transparency

Ray Dalio, the founder of Bridgewater Associates, advocates for stringent mindfulness practices within the organization. His philosophy of "Radical Transparency" encourages employees to confront their weaknesses and mistakes openly, promoting growth and communication.

This unique blend of financial acumen and mindfulness-based philosophy has resulted in Bridgewater being one of the world's largest hedge funds. Dalio's philosophy comes to life in the company's deliberate approach to decision-making, where reactions to short-term market trends are replaced by careful planning and strategy.

11.4. A Tale of Mindful Survival: Lehman Brothers' Minority

The 2008 financial crisis brought down multiple financial powerhouses, one of the most notable being Lehman Brothers. The institution's downfall was primarily due to its massive portfolio of securities tied to the US housing market.

However, amidst the chaos, some traders expressed mindfulness in response to the situation. Recognizing the signs of an impending crash, they moved to divest from the volatile housing market or invest in safeguarding alternatives.

These examples showcase a level of calm and strategic thinking in a frantic, high-stakes setting - a true embodiment of mindfulness in action.

11.5. Conclusion: The Mindful Navigation Method

Each of these stories highlights the effectiveness of mindful investing. They demonstrate that by maintaining calm amidst chaos, focusing on long-term goals, adopting a measured pace of decision-making, and building a transparent and open environment, investors can successfully navigate the volatility of financial markets.

Adopting these lessons into your investing journey may not guarantee success, but it will undoubtedly help to transform the experience of investing from a frantic race to a balanced journey of growth and discovery. With each investment, you slowly build not just your financial portfolio, but your financial wisdom, patience, and resilience.

Remember, just as each company has its unique vision and values, your investment journey should be tailored to match your financial goals, risk tolerance, and personal philosophy. Let these case studies be your guiding beacon as you embrace your own mindful journey through the financial markets.